Travel Light, Travel Smart

Pack Less and See More of the World

A MINIMALIST TRAVELING GUIDE

By Michael D. Haus

Table of Contents

Ten Reasons for Traveling Light... 4

Travel Bag Tactics and Tips 13

Cutting Down on Trip Clothing 25

Protecting Your Documents 39

Trimming Down Toiletries 46

Traveling With Technology 62

Fitting Things in Your Bag 66

Traveling Light for Couples 73

Ten Reasons for Traveling Light

If you wish to travel far and fast, travel light.

Cesare Pavese

"Is that all your stuff?"

Nodding "yes" to that question, or better yet, smirking in response, is one of my favorite pastimes. Together with many other minimalists, I love traveling light.

Most people take enough stuff on the weekend to last a year. Then there are people like me.

Why are we minimalists so bent on traveling light? The reasons are many:

Reason #1: Conserving energy for what really counts

If you've ever felt worn out after lugging a 60-liter backpack around all day, imagine how many more sights you could see—or how much fresher your legs would feel—if your backpack weighed 20 (or even 40) liters instead.

Next time you watch someone try to muscle their treasure of earthly goods into the overhead baggage area of a plane or onto a crowded bus, you can be doubly thankful for the Spartan pack by your side.

Reason #2: Less to lose

Regardless of the nature of your trip or how you arrive, it's nice not to have to worry about whether your luggage will also arrive. Keeping things simple leaves you with less to carry; it also means less to lose.

Most veteran travelers have at least one horror story of luggage turning up three weeks late or not at all.

If you have a favorite necklace or heirloom watch you can't bear to lose, the best strategy is to either keep it on your body or leave it at home. Nothing can be misplaced by baggage handlers because there's nothing for them to handle.

Reason #3: Stress reduction

Traveling can be stressful at the even best of times, and lugging a huge piece of baggage adds to that stress. Taking a larger rucksack and too much gear is the most common mistake for first time or rookie travelers.

Bottom line: travelling light is simply a more stress-and-hassle-free way to go. You have more time, because packing takes little. You waste less energy hauling stuff. You know what you have, where everything is, and that it's sufficient—so there is much less to worry about.

Reason #4: You can pack fast!

Want to leave for a trip at the drop of a hat? Some travelers have that down to such a science that they can leave within 30 minutes—or less—of when they decide to set off. That sort of speed comes in handy when you're moving from place to place.

Light travelers can also avoid having to "drop off" the suitcases before starting to explore, or easily make unplanned stops along the way.

And when they get off the plane, there's no waiting around to collect luggage because it's been with them all the time.

Reason #5: It's more secure

Lighter bags translate into a much reduced need to hand over your belongings to the care of others, which in reduces the chances of theft, damage, misrouting or other baggage handling mistakes by airlines, railroads, or bus lines. Similarly, you foil those who would enlist your unsuspecting aid as a conveyor of contraband goods.

Reason #6: You can blend in more easily with the locals

By bringing fewer items of clothing and making those ones that can be worn in many different situations you are less likely to find yourself over or underdressed.

The key here is versatility (e.g. steer clear of duds that are flashy or trashy). Unfortunately, clothes specifically designed for travel (such as cargo shorts or pant legs that zip off to become shorts) don't always fit in. If you're not sure what most people wear in your chosen destination, Google to learn what you can.

Also, nothing says "I am a tourist" quite like two suitcases and a carry-on bag. Packing light will help you to dodge that label.

Reason #7: You will save money

On a flight to Auckland with Air New Zealand, one traveler was surprised by a $75 "excess baggage" fee for a single 17-kilogram piece of luggage. In the past, they never had to pay for carry-ons with that particular airline.

Extra baggage fees, which are hitting us from many airlines now—$25 down the drain here, $90 down the drain there—really do add up.

"Welcome to the wave of the future," say industry experts. When airlines started charging for checked baggage, many travelers cut down to carry-ons. Now that charges often apply to carry-ons as well, it's time for minimalist travelers to fight back with even less luggage.

The less you pack the more money you'll save, and you won't have to pay porters to carry luggage at hotels or airports.

You'll also have an easier time traveling via public transportation, which will cut down on expensive cab fees. If you pack light enough, you might even be able to walk (which is good exercise, too!).

Reason #8: You will save time

Packing light allows for greater mobility. You won't need to arrive at airports as early, and you'll be among the first to leave the airport after your arrival while others wait at baggage claim.

Even if you do decide to check in some extras, keeping essentials and valuables with you on the plane is a good way to make sure you aren't left high and dry if your luggage does take a detour.

Reason #9: Packing light is fun!

Seeing how many items can be eliminated from a backpack or suitcase can be quite a puzzle, and a fun one at that. The key is to focus on how many things can be left out without too much hassle. This is in sharp contrast to the RV-packing mindset, where the goal is to bring everything you might possibly need.

Reason #10: Packing Light is Green

Traveling light is an important part of an environmentally friendly lifestyle—one which results in lower fossil fuel consumption and fewer vehicles required for transportation. The less you take on trips, the more you are helping to preserve the Earth for others to enjoy.

In conclusion:

Traveling light is simply a better, more hassle-free way to go: you'll expend less energy by not hauling a heavy bag and less time searching through multiple bags to remember where you put that city map!

With less to pack up at the end of your vacation, you can squeeze every last memorable moment out of your trip.

Ultimately, you'll spend less time worrying and more time enjoying. You will also be following the advice of Antoine de Saint-Exupery, a famous aviator of the early 20th century, who once said:

He who would travel happily
must travel light.

Travel Bag Tactics and Tips

*The first commandment of adventurers everywhere,
"Thou shalt not travel with anything thou cannot carry
at a dead run for half a mile and store under thy
seat."*

Erma Bombeck

I ain't takin' nothin' that'll slow down my travelin' ...

Johnny Cash

Before planning what to bring on your trip, it's important to pick the best backpack or suitcase for your needs.

Choosing a smaller bag is the first step towards avoiding that largest of mistakes (bringing too much stuff). It is also a way to automatically limit what you bring along.

The key is to find a bag that you can be happy with over an extended period of time.

Suitcase or Backpack?

Whether you bring a suitcase or backpack depends on the nature of your trip.

Suitcases are more likely to be useful if you:

- will be "headquartered" in one motel while you tour the countryside
- have a myriad of things that you really do need to take (too much for a backpack)
- have no need to keep things with you during the day
- will be traveling by car (rather than public transportation)

In contrast, backpacks:

- work particularly well if you are staying at a new location each night
- encourage more efficient packing
- provide increased security
- speed up the packing process

Packing everything in a backpack also means limiting yourself to one bag, an exercise seen as a virtue by many seasoned travelers.

Benefits of One Bag

Traveling with one bag most likely means that you will:

- worry less about your things
- be more comfortable walking around
- save your back, and
- have a happier trip

The one bag you take could be a carry-on with wheels instead of a backpack. However, even in situations where a suitcase would be perfectly fine, many minimalist travelers simply prefer a backpack.

Skip the Wheels

Travel bags with wheels are nearly three times as heavy as bags the exact same size without wheels. In addition, the bag with wheels often results in a loss of up to a third—or even half—of available packing space.

So travelers pay triple the weight penalty in fees for rolling carry-ons if the bag is checked in, all for the use of wheels that can only be used in the smooth corridors of airports and hotels.

The minute you get out in the real world, bumping down cobblestone streets—or worse yet, unpaved roads with unpleasant organic materials strewn between ruts, the wheels quickly lose their value.

What Size Bag?

Suitcases: If you do opt for a suitcase and are flying to your destination, stick with a smaller size so you don't have to check in your bag.

Many airlines now have limits of 45 inches for bags—length plus depth plus width.

Sometimes they allow for a little larger than this, but not much.

Backpacks: As long as your loaded backpack weighs less than 40-45 liters you should be fine. If your backpack is much bigger than that, you may face extra airline fees or have trouble squeezing onto crowded busses. Some bus drivers also charge extra if they think a backpack is too big.

Because backpacks are the bag of choice for most minimalist travelers, the remainder of this chapter will focus on backpack selection.

Choosing a Backpack Type

There are two basic types of backpacks, both of which have their place in the right situation:

Top-loading packs, just as the name implies, open on the uppermost side. Because they hold more, top-loading packs are generally better for longer trips.

On the down side (no pun intended), their top-loading feature does make it more difficult to access items at the bottom of the pack.

Front-loading packs, of the type commonly used by school children, generally feature a zipper that opens up the entire front side.

While this feature allows users to access anything in the pack very quickly, it also puts a lot of stress on the zipper. That's why front-loading packs are generally used only for day or weekend trips.

Backpack Features to Look For

In selecting a backpack, there are a couple of important features to be aware of.

Though many minimalist travelers have moved in the direction of small tablet computers such as the iPad, some still require a laptop. If you do need to carry your laptop, look for a pack with a laptop pocket.

A "rain fly" is another helpful feature of some of the newer packs. In the event of rain, these backpack covers slide easily over the pack, protecting your gear from moisture. A rain fly is highly recommended—especially if you are traveling through Southeast Asia or other tropical places where heavy rains are particularly common.

Other backpack features to look for would include:

- comfortable shoulder straps
- a padded hip belt (to spread the weight of the pack)
- plenty of outside pockets

Other than the above, don't dwell too much on the features of the pack. The most important thing is to find one that's comfortable for you.

Although online shopping certainly has its benefits, the best strategy here is to go to a camping or sporting goods store such as Cabela's and start trying on packs.

Because no two people are built exactly the same, every person appreciates backpacks in their own unique way. Finding a backpack that fits comfortably can make a world of difference during your travels.

Backpack Brands

There are some places in life where you shouldn't cut corners: a backpack is one of those places. Though it's possible that you might stumble on the perfect pack for you at a garage sale or in Aunt Millie's attic, don't count on it.

Especially for extended trips, you'll want to look at the more expensive brands. Otherwise you risk being marooned in Malaysia with a zipper broken on your main compartment…

A quality backpack is likely to cost you $100 or more. Although the most popular backpack brand right now is Osprey, there are many other good brands. Here is the short list of backpack brands to check out:

- Osprey
- Arc'teryx
- Deuter
- GoLite
- Gregory
- Kelty
- Mountain Hardware

Traveling With Your Backpack

In addition to the task of finding the very best backpack for you, there are a few things to look out for when traveling with a pack.

Checking your backpack at an airport can be stressful because there is a risk of damage to the pack. Packaging your backpack properly can greatly reduce the risk—and fear—of damage.

There are two main ways to protect your backpack if you do need to check it in:

1. Place the pack in a larger duffel bag, or
2. Secure the protruding parts of the backpack with extra straps.

Duffel Bag Method: Duffel bags designed specifically to protect backpacks during travel can be purchased in outdoor specialty stores.

Put a TSA-approved lock on the backpack zippers when packing it in. This should keep your bag secure during the airport baggage-check process.

Straps Method: For this method, it is important that your backpack is filled. That's because the straps can better secure a backpack that has little extra fabric or room to move.

If you use this method, there won't be anything between your backpack and the conveyor belts used to move luggage in airports—so you have to cinch it up well.

Start by securing all the straps and buckles that are part of your pack. Allow as few free hanging items as possible. Tuck loose straps into zippered pockets or tie them to loop holes on the pack.

You will likely need 2-3 extra straps for this method. Those extra straps can be pulled around the protruding parts of the backpack (such as the shoulder straps or hip belt). If tightened properly, the extra straps will prevent the pack from getting snagged on conveyor belts.

Square knots are a good way to secure the extra straps—just be sure to pull them tight and tuck in any extra strapping.

Conclusion

Traveling light is a simple and exciting way to see other parts of the world—and of the available choices, a light, comfortable, and easily-organized backpack is one of the best pieces of gear a traveler bent on traveling light can acquire.

Being mobile, or able to carry everything you've got, is the key to easy foreign travel. If you think you're strong, try picking up all your equipment and walking around the block.

Paul Heussenstamm

The day on which one starts out is not the time to start preparations.

Nigerian proverb

Cutting Down on Trip Clothing

Own only what you can carry with you: know language, know countries, know people. Let your memory be your travel bag.

Aleksandr Solzhenitsyn

Think in terms of what you can do without—not what will be handy on your trip. When in doubt, leave it out.

Rick Steves

The bulk of even a minimalist traveler's luggage generally involves clothing. As a result, cutting down on trip clothing is one of the best ways to efficiently travel light.

Packing only two pairs of pants and three T-shirts could easily slash the weight (and size) of your luggage.

The downside is that you will have to wash your clothes more often, but you can accomplish that at a hostel in the evening instead of spending precious hours at the laundry mat.

When considering what to bring, it pays to consider the climate and culture of your destination, not to mention the reason for your trip. Attending a formal wedding calls for quite a different wardrobe than a week in the Australian outback. Similarly, those "Cuddle Duds" that keep you so warm in Finland won't be much good in Bermuda.

The first step in packing clothes is a paradigm shift in thinking. Instead of bringing everything you might possibly want to wear, your new mantra should be to bring only what you absolutely need.

Also, instead of a variety of outfit combinations, try bringing just two of each item: one to wear until it is dirty and one to change into. That's it: one in use, one on standby.

In terms of color, bring neutral-colored clothes that look fine in any combination. Zebra stripes and tie-die fluorescents are best left at home!

Following are some tips on what clothing to pack, piece by piece.

Pants and Shorts

The bulkiest and heaviest area of clothing is pants. The key here is to find pants (and clothing in general) that:

- wicks sweat (that means it picks up sweat from the skin and "wicks" it to the outside of the shirt where it can evaporate so you don't become chilled)
- keeps you warm even when wet
- dries quickly
- doesn't hold odors easily (e.g. stink!)
- takes a beating from daily washes, and
- still looks fashionable enough for any occasion

Cotton clothing can't accomplish those feats, which is why most people consider jeans and cotton T-shirts to be a poor choice.

Most travelers consider jeans to be unnecessary—they are heavy, large, and take forever to dry. Blue jeans are especially unpleasant in humid climates such as Asia and South America.

There are times when jeans would seem appropriate. Travelers who are climbing mountains in a colder part of South America may find jeans to be just the ticket. But if you want the warm, quick-wicking, dry-quickly, lightweight pants, try cargo pants with pockets instead.

Shorts are not acceptable public attire in some cultures where they are considered ratty and unprofessional. In such places, no matter how hot, shorts simply aren't worn except for swimming. For this reason, a second pair of pants (rather than one pair of pants and one of shorts) is often a must.

Skirts

In some cultures women wear mostly—or only—skirts. For women traveling to such cultures, it pays to make note of the customs well in advance.

If skirts are required or needed at least some of the time, look for ones that wrinkle-free skirts with the same qualities you might look for in pants. In some cultures "skorts" (a combination of a skirt and shorts) might be a viable option to also consider.

Shirts

Some minimalists have only two shirts to their name. This makes deciding what to wear incredibly easy.

"What shirt should I wear today?"

"The one I didn't wear yesterday!"

Though cutting down to just a few shirts might seem challenging, experienced minimalists say that once they get used to the simplicity, the complexity that others consider "normal" becomes the audacious thing.

If you really want to pack light, take two shirts, maybe three. Cotton is not recommended: cotton shirts absorb water easily and also take longer to dry than their synthetic counterparts.

You'll also want to stay away from sweaters and other fluffy or bulky shirts that take up too much room.

If you wish to purchase a souvenir shirt while on the road, packing fewer makes even more sense. Be aware that there aren't many shirts available for big or tall people in Asia, and not as many shirts for short people in the Scandinavian countries.

Underwear

One clothing item worth investing is ExOfficio underwear. Widely considered by travelers to be both high-performance and low-maintenance, these underwear feature quick-drying fabric that allows travelers to wash on the go and pack fewer pairs.

In addition to being lightweight, ExOfficio underwear is quite comfortable. Here's a rundown of their technical advantages:

Quick Drying: Made primarily of nylon, these boxers dry much faster than typical cotton underwear. The fact that they can dry in hours means fewer pairs needed for trips.

Moisture Wicking: Without emphasizing the details, let me just say that ExOfficio underwear will keep you dry in the most important areas far more effectively than their cotton counterparts.

Odor Resistant: Even the most hygienic of us find it hard to stay fresh while traveling for months on end. ExOfficio underwear is treated to control odor-causing bacteria.

While that statement on the package that says "17 countries, 6 weeks, one pair of underwear" is rather ambitious, traveling the world is entirely doable with two pairs of these briefs.

Many world travelers who have tested ExOfficio undergarments in the field enjoyed them so much that they continued to use them after their trip was over.

One caveat: nylon melts rather easily, so never dry your ExOfficio underwear by setting them near to a fire. Even a conventional electric tumble dryer set to warm may inadvertently reduce your inventory of skivvies.

Footwear

Packing just a few pairs of shoes for a longer trip, especially one that encompasses a wide range of activities, can be a special challenge—especially since shoes are a matter of personal comfort and taste.

The ideal shoe would be flexible, lightweight, durable, and suitable for a variety of situations. Sandals are not accepted in some restaurants, though you might get by with close-toed sandals and socks.

Whether your shoe of choice is a loafer, black tennis shoe, or sandal, you'll want to minimize the number of shoes you take and try to wear (rather than pack) the heaviest pair.

Given their typical weight, bulk, and awkward shape, shoes are also a challenge to pack. It's usually best to pack a pair of shoes tightly together, soles out, with the heels at opposite ends.

Don't neglect the spaces inside your packed shoes: they're great for fragile items or anything else that will fit.

Jackets or Coats

While the type of jacket you select depends on where you are going, world travelers should look for a year-round, multi-season jacket—a coat that works for everything from shoveling snow to attending an opera.

A slim coat with linings or layers works well. The ideal coat would have a water-resistant shell for inclement weather, a middle-of-the-road version for fall and spring, and an extra warm liner (like a zip-out fleece) fit for Siberian winters.

For some destinations, you might also get away with wearing layers *instead* of bringing a jacket. This works well in moderate climates, where you can manage your body temperature simply by adding or shedding layers.

If there is a way to avoid bringing a jacket, you can save a lot of space, and, more importantly, weight in your travel bag.

Rain Gear or Umbrella

Another important item to bring is a small umbrella or a rain jacket—especially if you're visiting the tropics, a rain forest or, say, Seattle.

Socks

Travelers often spend big money on upgraded luggage yet only a few dollars on an item that is arguably a much more significant piece of travel gear: socks.

Because travel tends to involve a lot of standing and walking, a high percentage of one's physical comfort starts with the feet.

Fortunately, there is an impressive array of socks on the market to take care of this need. And, as footsore walkers soon learn, spending a bit more on socks is worth it—especially for travel.

There are numerous kinds of travel socks available that will dry extra fast if they get wet either outdoors or when you wash them. If you are in a warmer climate, consider socks with Merino Wool in them.

These therapeutic socks, which are knit with varying compression zones in the foot and leg, are designed to stimulate blood flow and reduce swelling. Wear a pair and your feet, ankles and legs will be less prone to feel tired and achy at the end of the day.

Stay away from cotton socks, which are not recommended for active wear. 100% cotton socks tend to absorb sweat, saturate quickly and dry slowly—a perfect recipe for blisters.

In terms of how many pairs of socks to bring, 2-4 pairs should do the job (depending on how often you plan to wash).

If you prefer sandals (and no socks at all), remember that some restaurants do not allow customers with open-toe sandals. You might get into some restaurants with close-toed sandals and dark socks, if that is your preference.

In your shoes and socks as with all clothing choices, the number one aim should be comfort, warmth, simplicity, durability and yes—space.

Comfort has its place, but it seems rude to visit another country dressed as if you've come to mow its lawns.

David Sedaris

Packing light is another key to travel pleasure ... Resolve to be a carefree traveler and not a harried clothes horse. You will cease being a prisoner of porters and taxicabs, forced to stay at the first hotel you see, unable to "shop around". If you have taken too little, you can always remedy the deficiency at the destination. But meantime, you will know a kind of travel ease that only light packing can bring about.

Arthur Frommer

Protecting Your Documents

A fool and his luggage are soon parted.

P-3 Orion aircraft crew slogan

I travel light; as light, that is, as a man can travel who will still carry his body around because of its sentimental value.

Christopher Fry

At home, the most important documents you carry in your wallet are most likely your driver's license and vehicle proof of insurance. When you travel abroad, however, there are a number of additional documents that you'll need to keep not only safe, but close at hand. Following is a short list:

- Passport
- Driver's license (local and international if you have one)
- Credit cards
- Tickets and itinerary

- Traveler's checks (together with serial numbers)
- Hotel and tour reservation info
- Travel insurance documentation
- Medical condition alerts
- Who to contact in case you are injured

The safest place to keep items that are really important is directly on your person. Your backpack, carry-on bag or purse won't be as secure since they aren't always under your control (e.g. travelers often lay baggage down while checking in at airports, shopping, eating, etc.)

Those periods of separation may be brief, but do put your baggage—and what's in it—at risk. For that reason, it's really not best to store anything you can't afford to lose in your backpack or carry-on bag.

Document Holders

Although there are a number of different types of holders available to your important documents, all are designed to hide valuables under your clothing.

Money belts, document pockets that hang by thin straps hung around your neck, inside pockets, and front pant pockets can all be good places to keep your important items.

Clever pickpockets still have ways of targeting documents hidden in the best of places, but the holders make their job harder. (Note: front pant pockets are generally a better place to tuck documents safely than rear pant pockets).

If your documents do get stolen (in spite of your best precautions), be sure to act quickly.

Following are some tips to help you prevent and/or minimize loss:

- Make several copies of all your important papers, front and back, before leaving home.
- Store several copies of each throughout your luggage.
- Leave one copy at home with a family member or friend, in case you are separated from all of your possessions.
- Scan all of the important documents and put them on two USB drives.

Although document copies won't have the same clout as originals, they can speed the process of replacing those that are lost.

If you lose credit cards, for example, the information on the copies can help you to quickly report the loss.

It's also important to keep a list of traveler's check serial numbers. Leave one copy with your family and pack the other list where you can access it easily.

Each time you cash a traveler's check, cross its serial number off the list. If any of the unused checks are lost or stolen, you'll know exactly which numbers belong to the missing checks.

USB Drives

Many people who travel light prefer a USB drive to a laptop or tablet. The benefits are enormous—the USB drive is lighter, cheaper, and less likely to be stolen than a laptop.

Your two USB drives (one in case the other is lost) are the best insurance against losing important info. Cheap and convenient, they will also allow you to access your important files at Internet cafes.

Several different kinds of USB drives are popular among travelers today. Some drives (such as the Kingston Digital Data Traveler DT4000) are encrypted.

An encrypted drive is preferable if you are not that tech savvy. You can accomplish the same level of data security, for about a third of the price, by purchasing an unencrypted drive and using software to encrypt the files yourself.

Encryption Software

There are several programs available that will encrypt the files on your USB flash drive.

TrueCrypt, the most popular, can't be used on computers without administrator privileges. Most Internet cafes won't allow you to have administrator privileges, making TrueCrypt *not* the best option unless you are bringing your laptop.

FreeOTFE (which stands for Free On-the-Fly-Encryption) is a better option if you don't carry your own computer. Keeping all the important information on your USB drive encrypted is extremely important.

Routinely plugging a USB drive into PCs at Internet cafes without encryption is almost an invitation to have your files covertly copied without your permission. Don't let that happen to you!

For the best security, keep one USB drive in your luggage and one on your person.

Travel light and you can sing in the robber's face.
Juvenal, Roman poet

To know what to leave out and what to put in; just where and just how, ah, that is to have been educated in the knowledge of simplicity.
Frank Lloyd Wright

Trimming Down Toiletries

Like a bag you unpack at the end of a trip,
And you're wondering why did I take all of this;
These things I don't need weigh me down ...

Nanci Griffith

In anything at all, perfection is finally attained not when
there is no longer anything to add, but when there is no
longer anything to take away.

Antoine de Saint-Exupéry

Packing light, leaving the laptop behind, and braving the world sans suitcases lends itself to a sense of independence and freedom that is previously unknown to many travelers.

If pressed on their packing habits, however, even the most minimalist travelers often admit that the last packing area to be affected was their personal items or toiletries.

Cutting down has become so common, however, that even many women have thrown out that "hey, I'm a girl!" excuse.

This is not to imply that they have given up on personal hygiene or are now wreathed in B.O. Rather, they have discovered new eco-friendly options that make packing toiletry items "light" much easier.

While hardcore minimalists who recommend that the only toiletry item needed is a toothbrush do exist and even thrive, it is possible to take along a reasonable hygiene list without filling a third of your bag. So, how should we choose toiletries for long-term travel that don't take up most of the space in our backpacks?

The first "item" to eliminate is the fear that you won't be able to pick up certain items in a foreign country. If you're heading anywhere that's inhabited by other humans, chances are they also use hygienic products as well. If the destination civilization really is so remote that they don't worry about hygiene, there's no reason to keep up such a strict routine yourself.

One traveler to Tchad, Africa, remarked that he had often ridden a motorcycle in the sweltering heat wedged between two very sweaty (and equally smelly) locals. Realizing that no amount of deodorant would improve his lot, he quickly adapted the old adage "if you can't beat 'em, join 'em."

If you are a woman, try simplifying your beauty routine before the trip. Do you really need that eyelash curler to survive? How about that all that makeup, hairspray, or nail polish? Travelers of both sexes—what about that shaving cream? Go through your products and figure out what you're able to do without.

With that said, it is O.K. to allow one or two personal luxuries in your travel pack— especially when you are leaving so many behind. For some, just the smell of a favorite moisturizer has been said to stave off even the meanest bout of homesickness...

If you must, pick one luxury item. Then promise yourself there will be no more compromises. For everything else:

1. Think long and hard about whether or not you really need it,
2. Question if you could buy it locally once you arrive, or
3. Consider whether you could replace it with a more travel-friendly item.

Just remember: you only need enough toiletries to stay (relatively) clean—not "camera ready" in the jungles of Brazil. As long as you don't stink, you're O.K.—and in some places it's even all right to stink.

A list of "essential" toiletries could be considerably longer than the one presented on these pages; it's the area most subject to personal inclination. With that said, here are some ideas regarding "essentials" to take—or not take—on your trip:

Contact Lenses

Hanging onto glasses, or a supply of daily contact lenses, can be hard to do. A better option would be laser eye surgery or monthly contacts that can be slept in. Just be sure to test the contacts for some time before leaving to ensure that all is well and your eyes are not irritated.

Dental Care

Tooth powder: A great space-saving alternative to toothpaste, tooth powder saves space, reduces weight, risks fewer security hassles than pastes, and—most importantly—works great. Shaking tooth powder directly onto your toothbrush is likely to waste a bit; instead, dispense some into the cup of your palm then pick it up with a damp toothbrush.

Toothbrush and cap: A cap for your toothbrush will keep it clean, allow it to dry easily, and (if you get the type with an attached suction cup) hang from the nearest mirror or similar surface.

Dental floss: Rivaled only by the bandanna and duct tape for its multi-use potential, dental floss doubles as excellent heavy-duty thread which, in addition to mending, can be used for all kinds of tying chores (e.g. replacing a broken shoe lace, tying pant legs while riding a bike, securing plastic over a bottle that has no top, and the list goes on).

Floss also makes a superb slicing tool for items as diverse as cheese, birthday cake, and cold butter. Other emergency uses include as a clothesline, ukulele string, and quick fix for a broken toilet tank chain. With a little ingenuity, you can even use it to halt the drip of a leaky faucet. This is all in addition to cleaning your teeth.

51

Takeaway point: if you are traveling to the remote corners of the earth, don't forget floss!

Deodorant

If you want to cut out deodorant entirely, a plant-based diet really lends itself to less stinky sweat. Perspiration does still occur, but in a much less odorous fashion.

If you'd like to avoid gels or liquid deodorant, try baking soda. Rub a little on your armpits while they are still damp from the shower, and test the results.

You may be surprised to find how well it works. Not only will your "pits" stay fresh and dry all day, they will actually feel clean. Baking soda also works well as a cleansing agent for household use.

Deodorant crystals (mineral salts that inhibit underarm bacterial growth) are another good option. Being neither liquid nor gel, they need not be packed in a transparent baggie.

Ear Plugs

If you've ever been the lucky seat partner of a very annoyed baby and its worn-out mother, or with an incessantly snoring travel buddy, or worse yet—in a hostel room next to an impassioned couple that succumbs to the not-so-unthinkable, you will thank your lucky stars for a set of good plugs. Don't leave home without 'em. Better yet, take a spare.

Hair Care

Dry Shampoo: Spray it in, comb it out. It's really that easy to erase greasy shine when you use dry shampoo. If you're hiking a trail for five days with no shower access, dry shampoo is a great rescue option. While not the same as washing, it does leave hair feeling softer and much, much cleaner.

Electric razor/beard trimmer: The easiest solution for men is to grow a beard while on the trip. Disposable razors can also be purchased at most destinations, and a pair of blunt scissors designed for babies can be quite effective at trimming beards and moustaches.

Shaving Oil: Good things do come in small packages: a half ounce container of shaving oil can last for up to 100 shaves, working wonders for men and women on even the most sensitive skin. Far superior to foams or gels, shaving oil offers a consistently smooth shave while reducing nicks and razor burn. It also leaves skin conditioned and moisturized. There is also no mess to clean up when finished! You simply use it instead of shaving cream. All you need is 5-7 drops for a softer, smoother shave.

Tip: To minimize body odor, consider trimming body hair before setting off. Guys may feel awkward trimming their "pits," but taking them down to a short length does make it harder for bacteria to thrive. The same type of strategy works with, umm...various other regions.

Hairspray, gels, and mousse: not recommended if you can avoid them! If you insist, check out the latest airline travel regulations and take the appropriate size(s).

Hair brush: To save space, consider a hair brush that folds in half or one that's combined with a mirror. Or (if you're a guy), shave your head...

Laundry-related Items

Aloksak: Ultra-light packing makes laundry a necessity. Since machine washing isn't always efficient (for small loads) or even available, you may need to wash clothes by hand.

Enter the "Aloksak," an awesome alternative to washing laundry in the sink. An Aloksak is basically a durable, completely waterproof, Ziploc®-like bag. Laundry can easily be done in 15 minutes using a 12"x12" Aloksak bag.

Washing clothes in an Aloksak bag is a simple process:

1. Toss your dirty clothes into the bag, making sure to leave enough room for water. (You may have to do more than one load, depending on the size of your bag and how many clothes you have).
2. Fill the Aloksak with enough water to soak the clothes.
3. Add 10 drops of Dr. Bronner's (or a similar) soap.
4. Knead the bag, with the clothes in it, for 2-3 minutes.
5. Leave the clothes sealed in the bag for another 10 minutes.
6. Take the clothes out of the bag and rinse them.
7. Hang them up to dry using your elastic clothesline.

The total time for this little exercise, which includes 10 minute of soaking, is about 15 minutes.

Pack-it Compression Bags: These large plastic Ziploc bags are perfect for holding wet or soiled clothing. Simply place the clothes in the bag, zip it up, then press hard enough to make the air come out the other end. The result is a "shrink-wrapped" bag of dirty laundry which will be small enough to fit in your luggage.

Sink Stopper: If you anticipate washing your clothes in a sink, a universal (flat) sink stopper may come in handy. In undeveloped countries, many sinks don't have plugs. A flat rubber jar opener can also double as a sink stopper.

Multi-use soap: Purchasing a multi-use soap can reduce the amount of liquid(s) you need to carry considerably. This is particularly helpful with the airline limitations in effect today.

Many seasoned travelers prefer Dr. Bronner's liquid soap, which can be used as shampoo, body wash, and laundry detergent. In addition, to being organic, Dr. Bronner's is vegetable-based, fair-trade, and biodegradable.

Other eco-friendly perks include the fact that the bottles (including paper) are 100% post-consumer recycled and the lack of funky foaming agents or preservatives in their soap.

Buy it in large bottles and fill smaller 3-ounce airline-approved bottles to pack in your carry-on. You won't need much: one 3-ounce bottle of Dr. Bronner's can last as much as a month, even when used for *everything*.

If you have trouble finding Dr. Bronner's, check your local health food store for an organic, vegetable-based soap. Outdoor or camping stores are another good place to look:

the "camping soap" they carry offers a good alternative option.

Towels

Microfiber towels wick up moisture efficiently, yet somehow manage to dry out about four times more quickly than a regular towel. With the ability to pack away to 1/8 the size of a regular towel, plus be six times lighter, they are a must for traveling ultra-light.

Though they might feel a bit strange at first (e.g. you might miss your big fluffy towel), their space saving and quick drying features more than make up for this lack. A dry microfiber towel can also work well as a blanket or folded up as a pillow, both of which are helpful on long bus trips or other situations where warmth and/or comfort are needed.

Some microfiber towel brands work better than others, so be sure to read reviews before making a purchase.

Vaseline

Works great as lip gloss, a soother for chapped lips, on eyelids for a gorgeous "wet" look (women!), or to combat problems with dry skin. Keep a pocket-size container in your bag at all times!

Wet wipes

After 24-hour long bus rides or 12-hour flights you will most definitely feel the need for "freshening up". A small pack of 20 wet wipes is perfect for that: it will also come in handy when you run into restrooms sans toilet paper.

Women's Hygiene Products

Moon Cup: One toiletry item that many women choose to bring is a menstrual cup, just in case "Aunt Flo" catches up with them on their travels. Because moon cups are reusable, they save weight and space.

Sense of Humor

This item should be at the top of your packing list regardless of category. It can get you through all sorts of situations, in addition to making travel (and life in general) a more enjoyable thing. When packing your bags, then, don't leave your chuckle behind!

From now on, I'm travelin' light.
Billie Holiday

Less is more.
Ludwig Mies van der Rohe

Traveling With Technology

Pack twice the money and half the gear.
Old vagabonding adage

On a long journey, even a straw weighs heavy.
Spanish Proverb

Though technology can be incredibly useful, it's best to leave much—if not all—of it behind when traveling light. It's so much easier to live in the moment when distractions are eliminated!

The list of electronic items that *could* be brought on a trip is overwhelming, to say the least. Cell phones, GPS devices, iPods, iPads, laptops, electronic book readers, tablet computers, external hard drives, and USB flash drives are just a few of the popular items.

As in all other packing list categories the secret is to traveling light with electronics is to bring fewer items that weigh less.

Travelers frequently save space and weight by bringing a tablet computer or an eBook reader instead of a full-sized laptop.

Though smaller, smartphones can also present a hassle.

Rule of thumb: If you spent $600 on your smartphone and will spend the trip worrying about losing it, it isn't worth bringing.

Many countries have cheap mobile phones that can be purchased. Pre-paid SIM, which will allow you to make and receive calls on a local number, are also available.

Unless the focus of your travel is to take professional pictures, you may want to leave the DSLR camera behind. Besides being a major pain to carry, larger cameras catch the attention of locals and alter their behavior. A small point-and-shoot will be far less intrusive. In addition, thieves are often on the lookout for DSLR cameras.

Most photographers that take thousands of raw photographs bring along multiple external hard drives. In order to travel light, two alternatives would be to bring along multiple flash drives or upload the files to Dropbox or Google Drive.

Because uploading files in an Internet café may go too slowly in 3rd world countries, bringing several USB drives might be a better choice. Currently there are 64GB USB hard drives for very affordable prices, and the capacity keeps growing as technology advances.

Though it's difficult to travel with the very minimum amount of technology, the fewer large or expensive items you bring on your trip, the less worrying you will do about theft and the more time you can spend enjoying your travels.

Once in a while it really hits people that they don't have to experience the world in the way they have been told to.

Alan Keightley

...

Travelin' light is the only way to fly.

J. J. Cale

Fitting Things in Your Bag

Wherever you go, there you are.
Your luggage is another story.

From a Japanese parable

Fitting everything in isn't just about what you pack—it's about how you pack as well. Putting a lot of things in a small space can be like a jigsaw puzzle. It can also be fun.

Following is an overview of some packing devices and/or schemes to help you on your way:

Packing Cubes

These rectangular zippered little pouches:

- feature mesh panels that reduce the weight of the bag and make the contents more visible
- contain various pockets that are very helpful in organization

Packing cubes work great for holding electronics, cords, cables, toiletries, and personal items. In addition to keeping all the items in your bag neatly contained, they promote organization in general.

In the words of one traveler, packing cubes help them to "always know where everything is, and keep the stuff that I don't need 'tucked away'." She found waiting for other travelers, and watching as they dug through their bags for things they couldn't find, particularly frustrating.

Your choice of cubes will depend on how you choose to organize things. Fortunately, the packing cubs do come in a number of sizes. If you need several cubes, going with different colors can help you to keep things straight.

Organizer Pouches

These flat, rectangular, nylon pouches contain several compartments and usually close with a zipper. They often include see-through mesh panels, making it easy to see exactly what's in the bag.

If money is an issue, Ziploc® bags can accomplish the same thing. Pouches are much more convenient and durable, however, and they are not that expensive. In addition to working well for toiletry items, many travelers have found the larger pouches to be handy for organizing their important papers or even clothes.

One bonus: using cubes or pouches increases the likelihood that your belongings will remain tidy and well organized should you be singled out for a search.

Stuff Sacks

Similar to packing cubes, stuff sacks are used to compress and compartmentalize clothes and other items. Stuff sacks are great for squeezing items such as jackets and beach towels down to manageable sizes.

Whether you prefer packing cubes to stuff sacks, or use cubes for some items and sacks for another, is a matter of personal preference.

Some travelers prefer stuff sacks over packing cubes for clothing items because the sacks compress better and also conform more easily into the contour of a backpack.

To minimize the space taken by clothes, roll them up tightly. Some travelers like to roll clothes up around a central object such as a shoe. Either way, rolling up clothes saves much more space than folding them because it naturally eliminates much of the extra air.

To conserve the most space, roll everything that can be rolled—jackets, towels, underwear, and anything else that can be rolled.

If you really prefer folding your clothes, a suitcase (rather than a backpack) might work better for you.

Ziploc® Bags

Budget-conscious travelers often organize toiletry items in Ziploc® bags. These clear little pouches make it so easy to see what's in each bag, and you can fit them all in larger bag away from your clothes.

Be sure to buy heavy duty bags. Cheap zipper bags tend to leak or break—something you don't want to have happen in the middle of Malawi!

In Conclusion

Efficient use of the space available is one of the keys to packing light, so watch out for— then utilize—any wasted space. For example, if you are packing an extra pair of shoes, stuff socks into them.

Packing your pack in an organized manner will help save space and time. It will also increase your awareness of everything in your pack, together with the chance that you will notice additional items that can be eliminated.

> *Pack less, and become unattached to possessions.*
> *And then ... pack less.*
>
> Jimmy Wales

Traveling Light for Couples

Make everything as simple as possible ... but no simpler.
Albert Einstein

Couples traveling together have a unique opportunity to save space by sharing different items.

Following is a short list of items that can easily be shared by minimalist-minded couples, lightening the load of each:

Binoculars

Camera(s) or lenses

Contact Lens Solution

Laptops or other technology

Laundry Supplies

Multi-purpose Soap

Toilet Tissue

Toothepaste

Deoderant

Use your imagination and think of what you can share to lighten your load.

Not recommended: toothbrushes or towels!

Note: the entire philosophy of traveling light is to carry less and replenish often. Certain items, when shared, will certainly be used up more quickly—so be prepared to make shopping trips more frequently in such cases.

The love of economy is the root of all virtue.
George Bernard Shaw

Made in the USA
Middletown, DE
25 September 2018